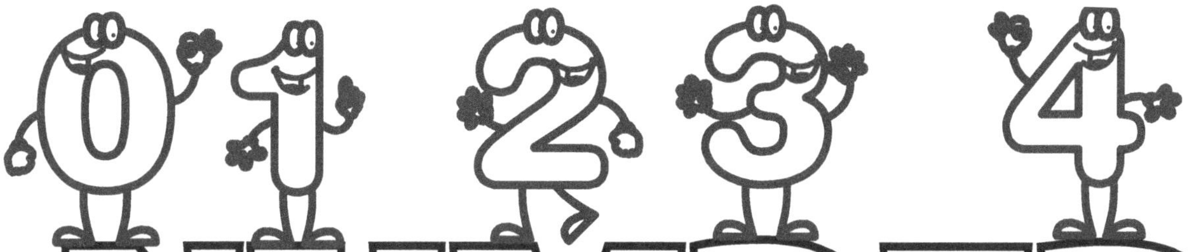

NUMBER COLORING BOOK

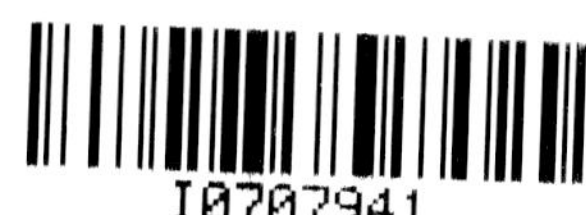

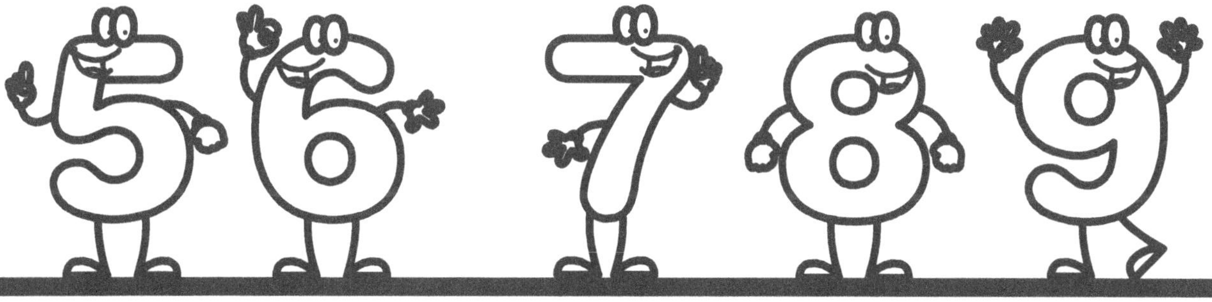

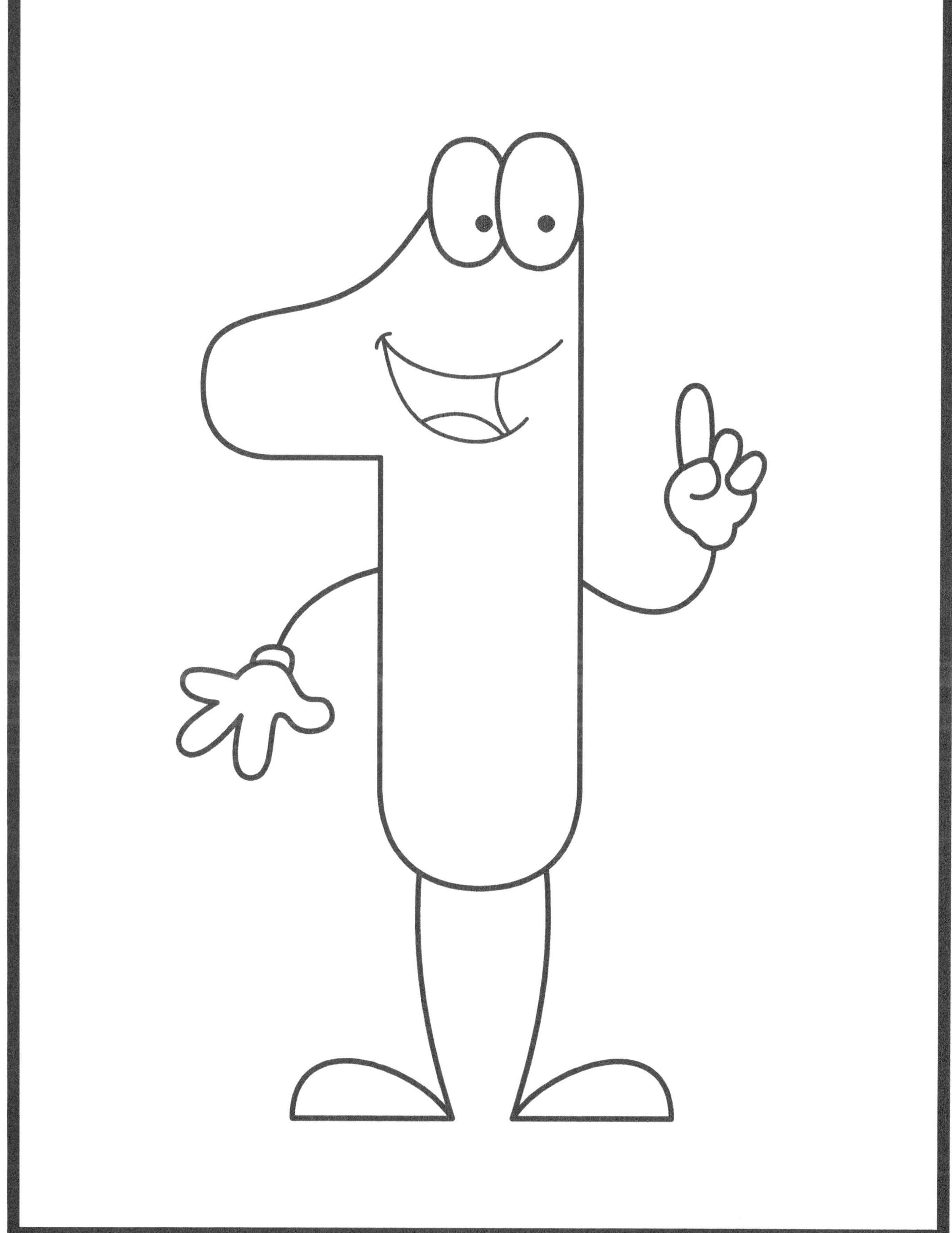

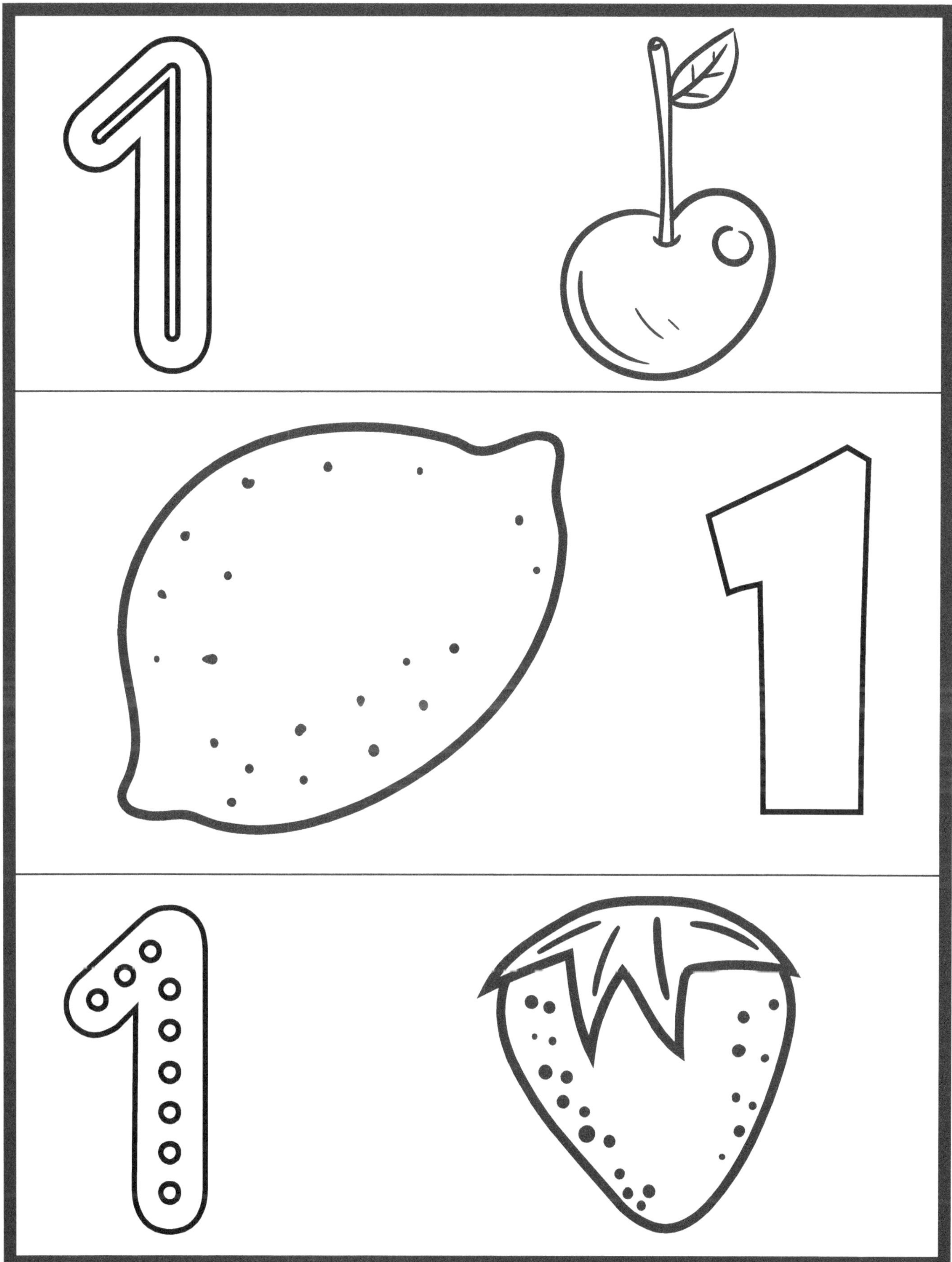

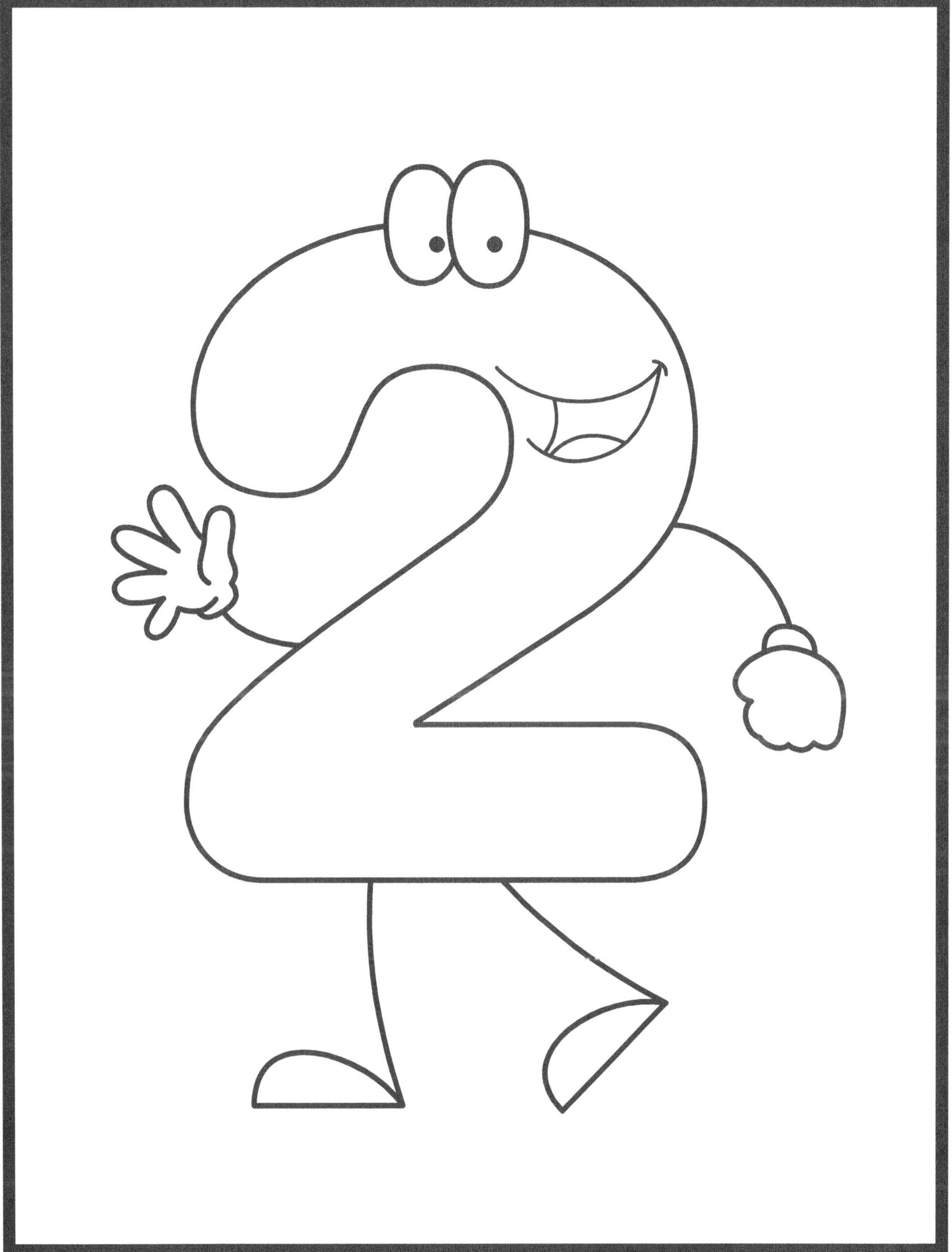

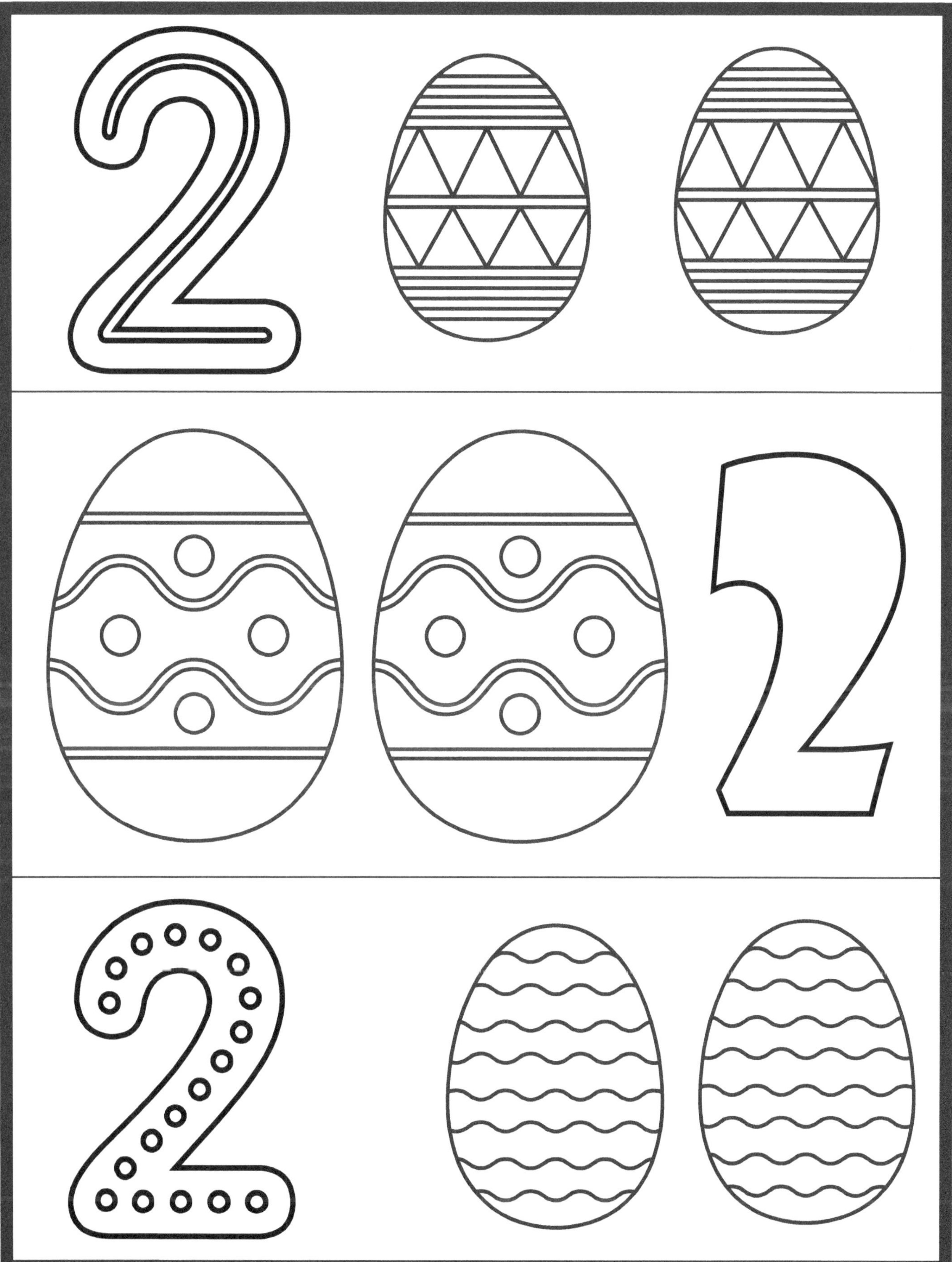

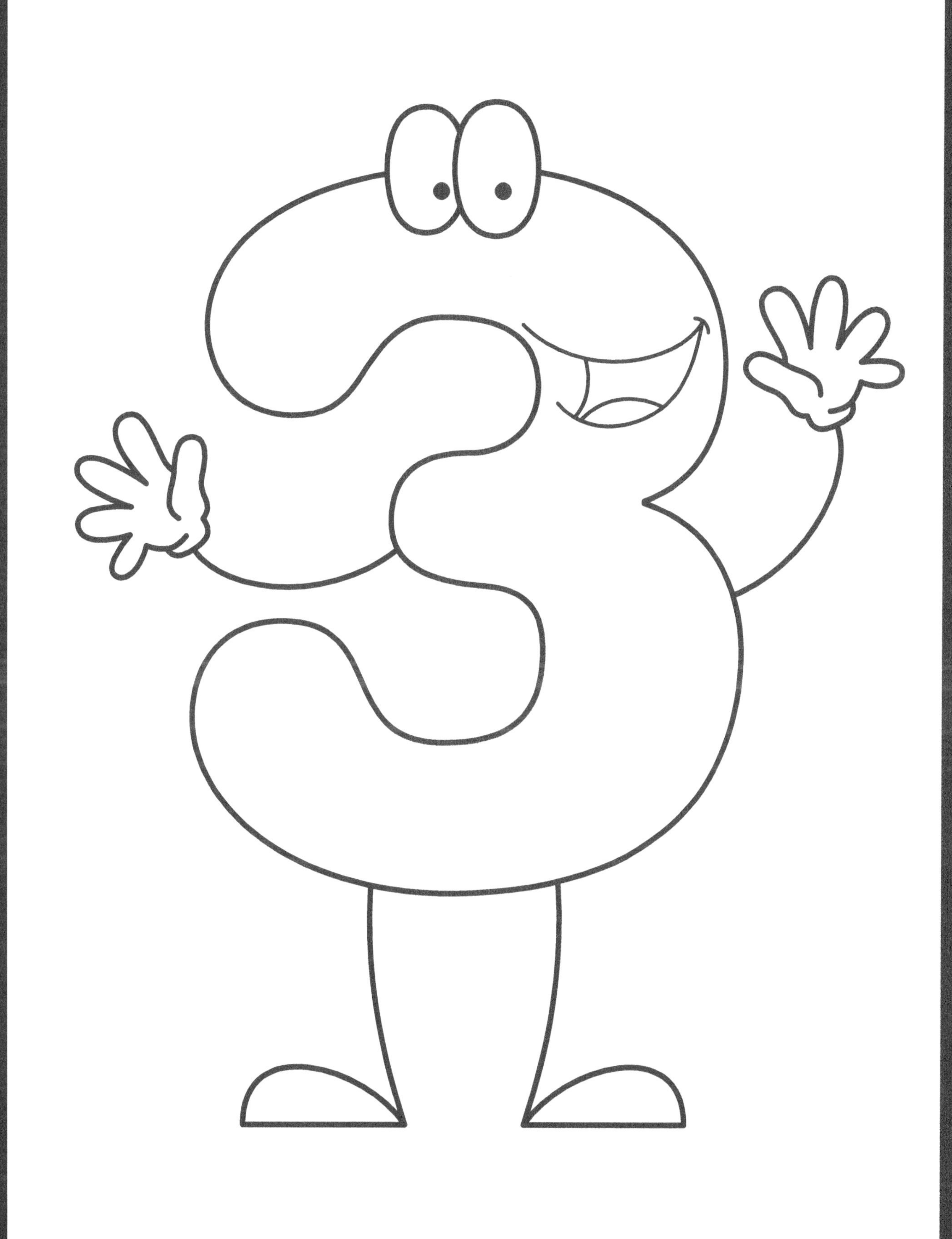

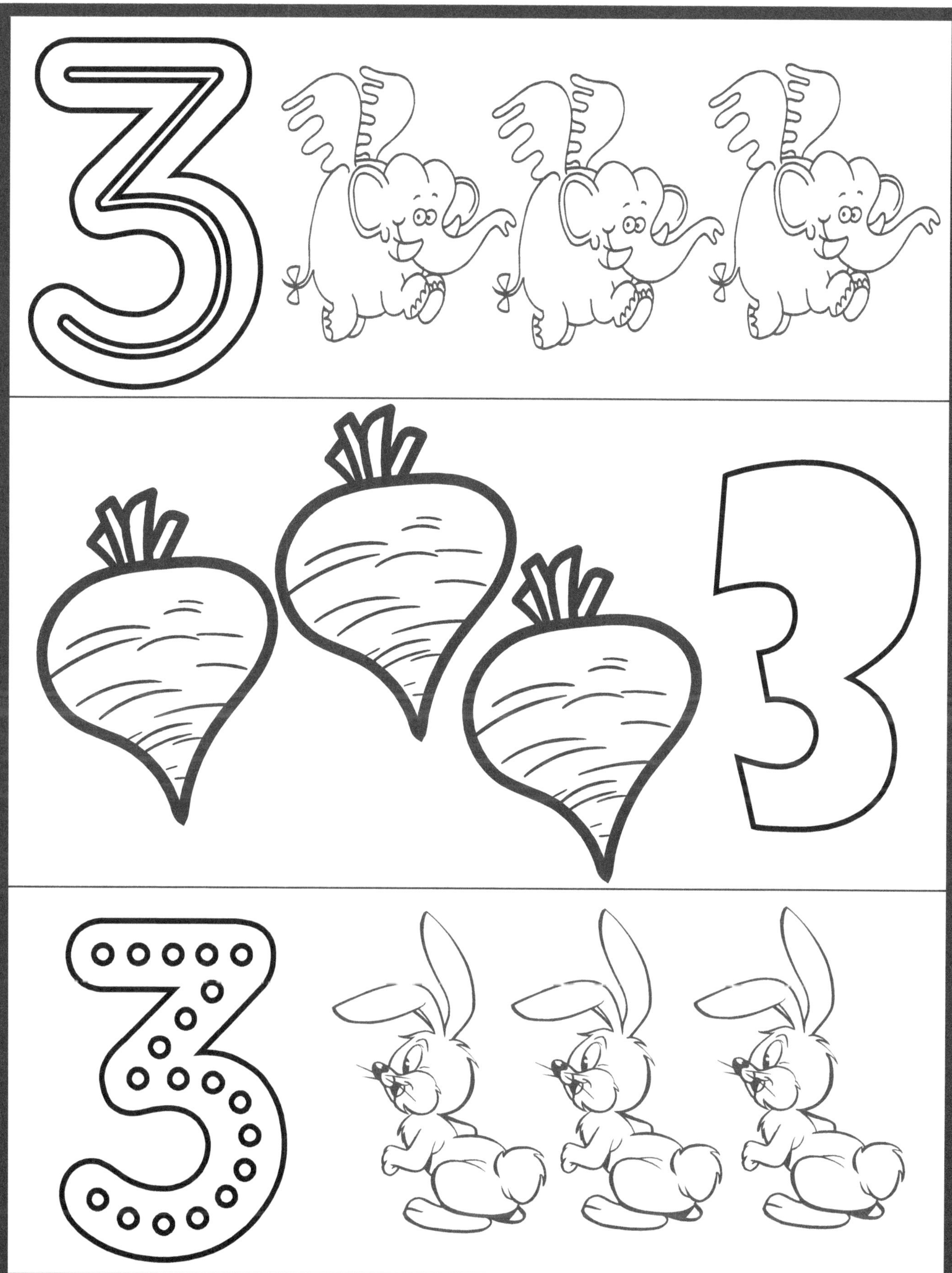

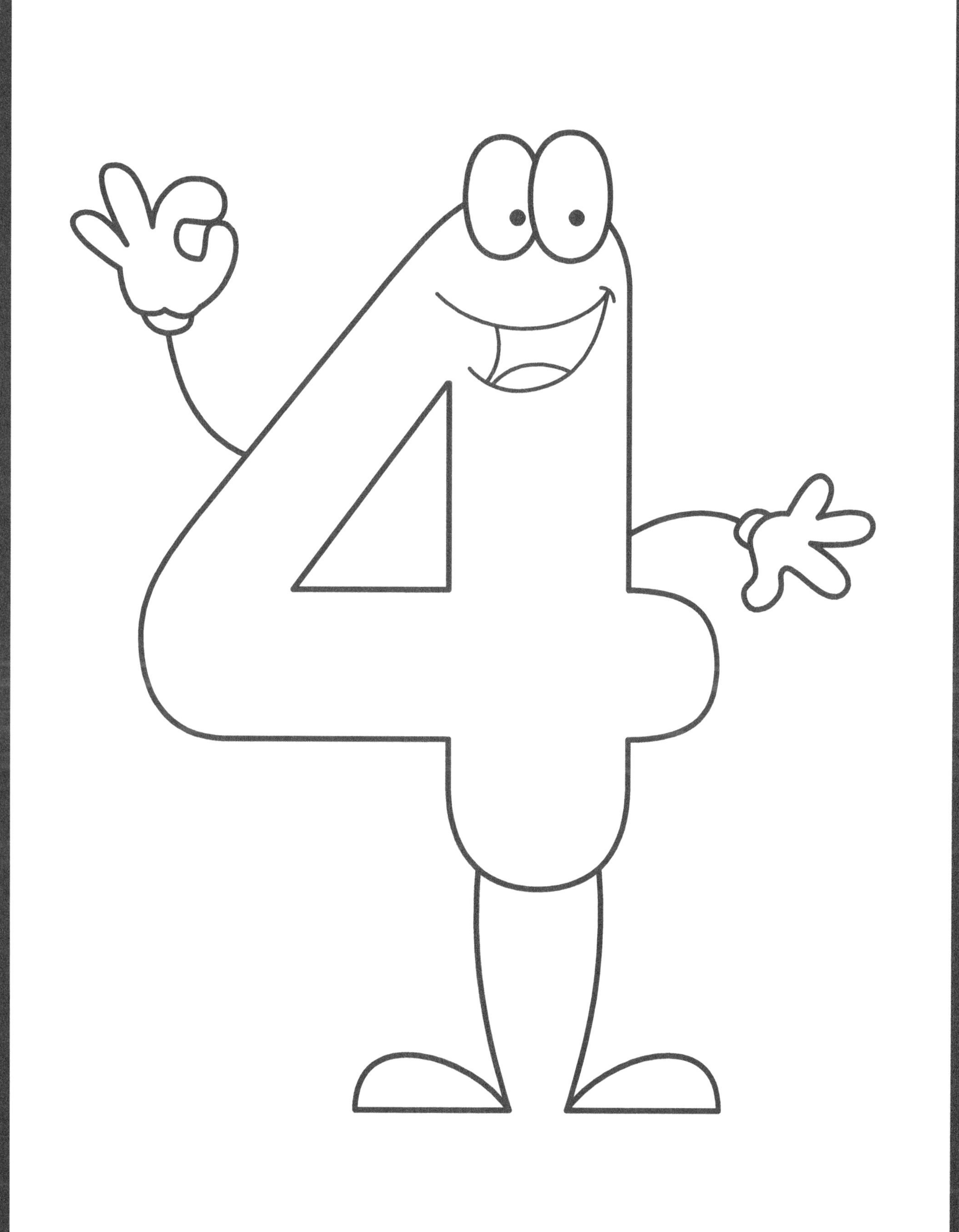

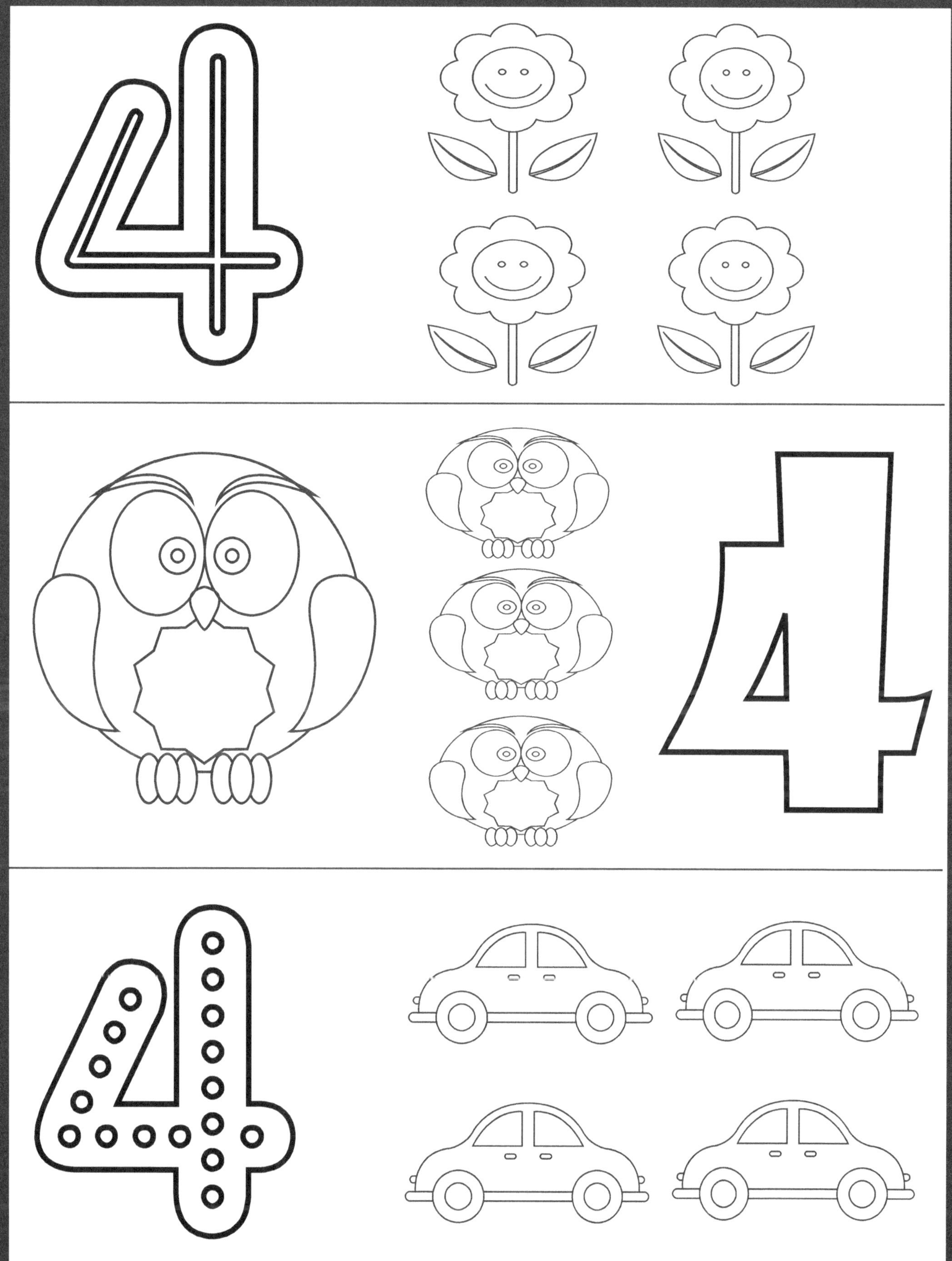

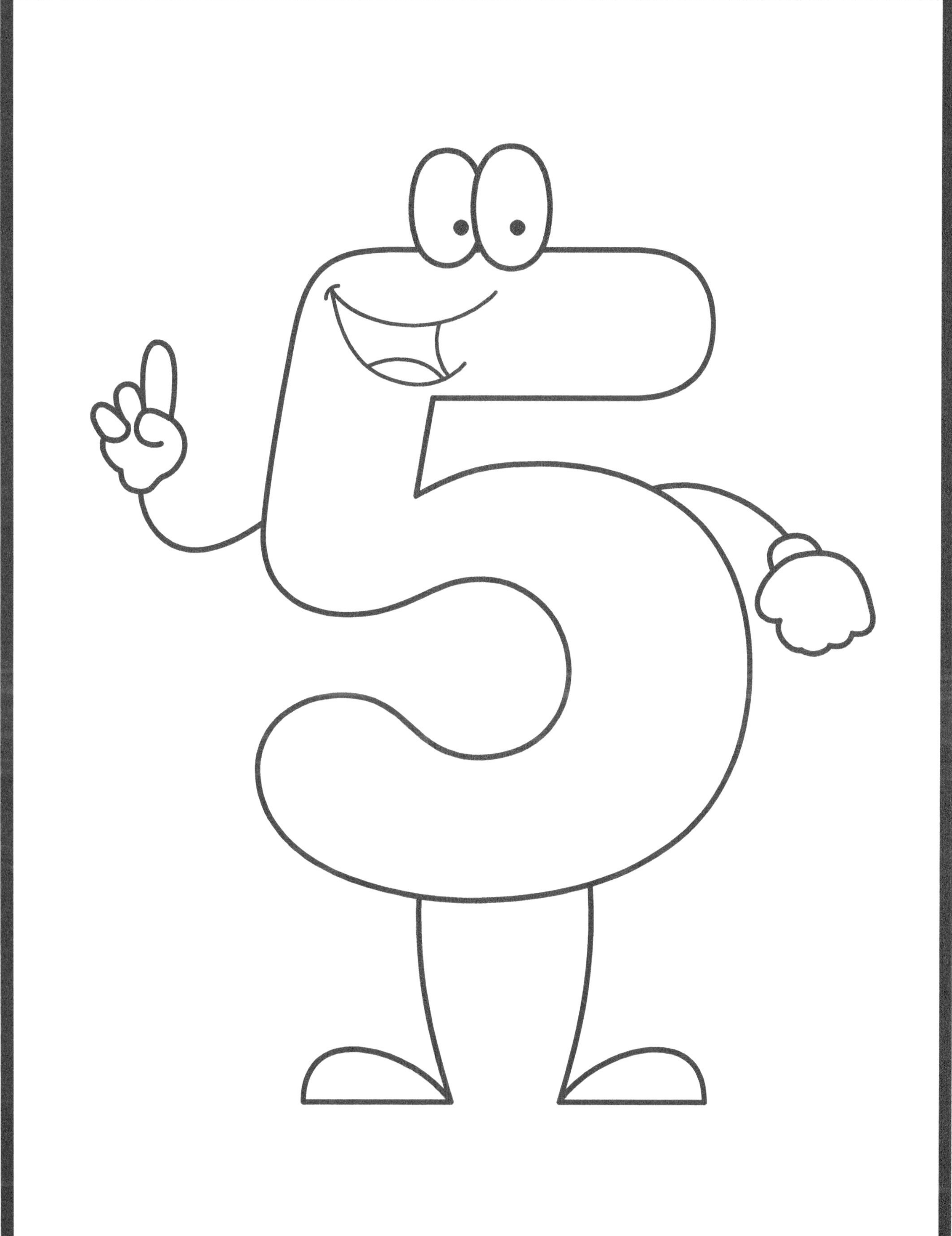

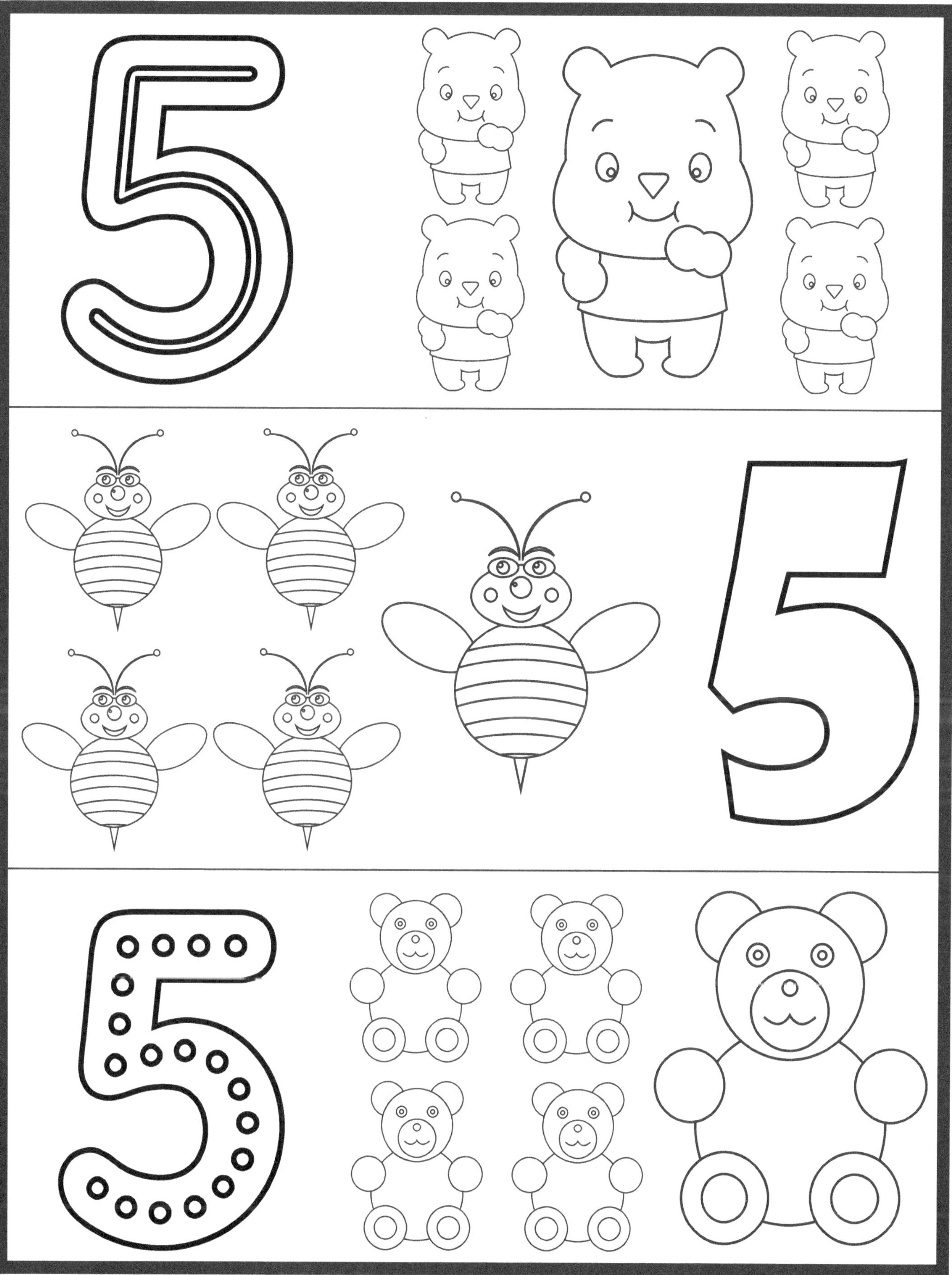

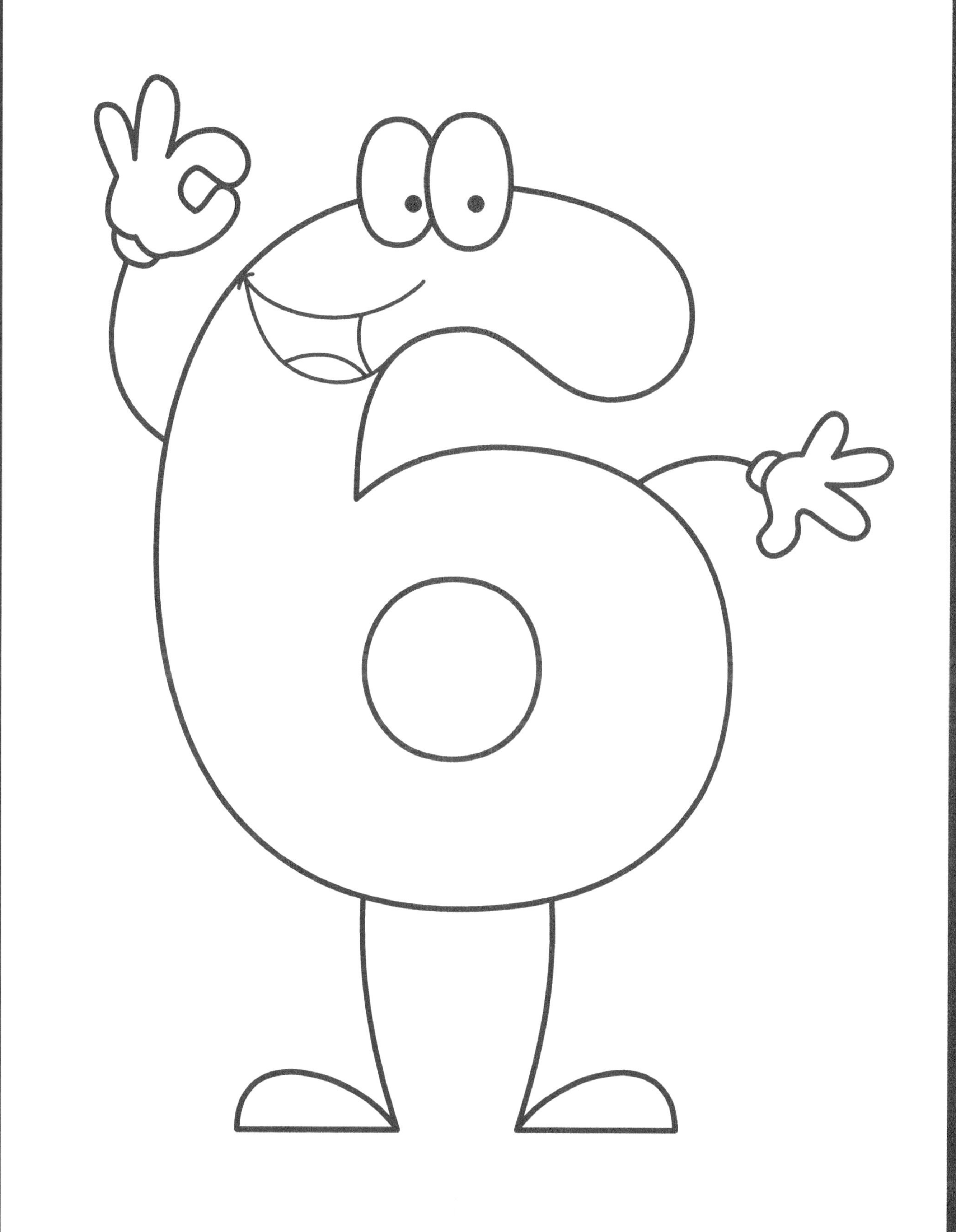

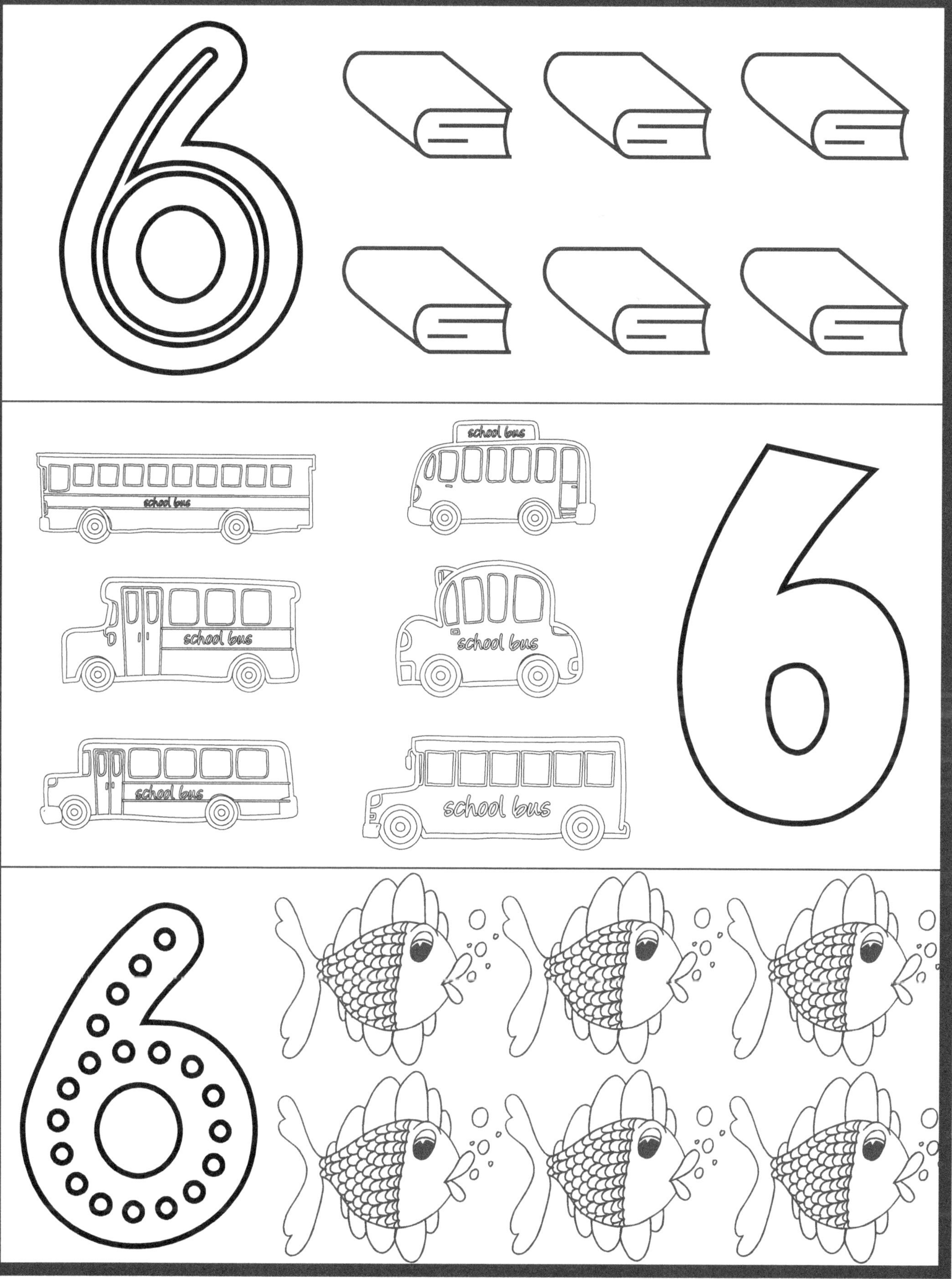

school bus
school bus
school bus
school bus

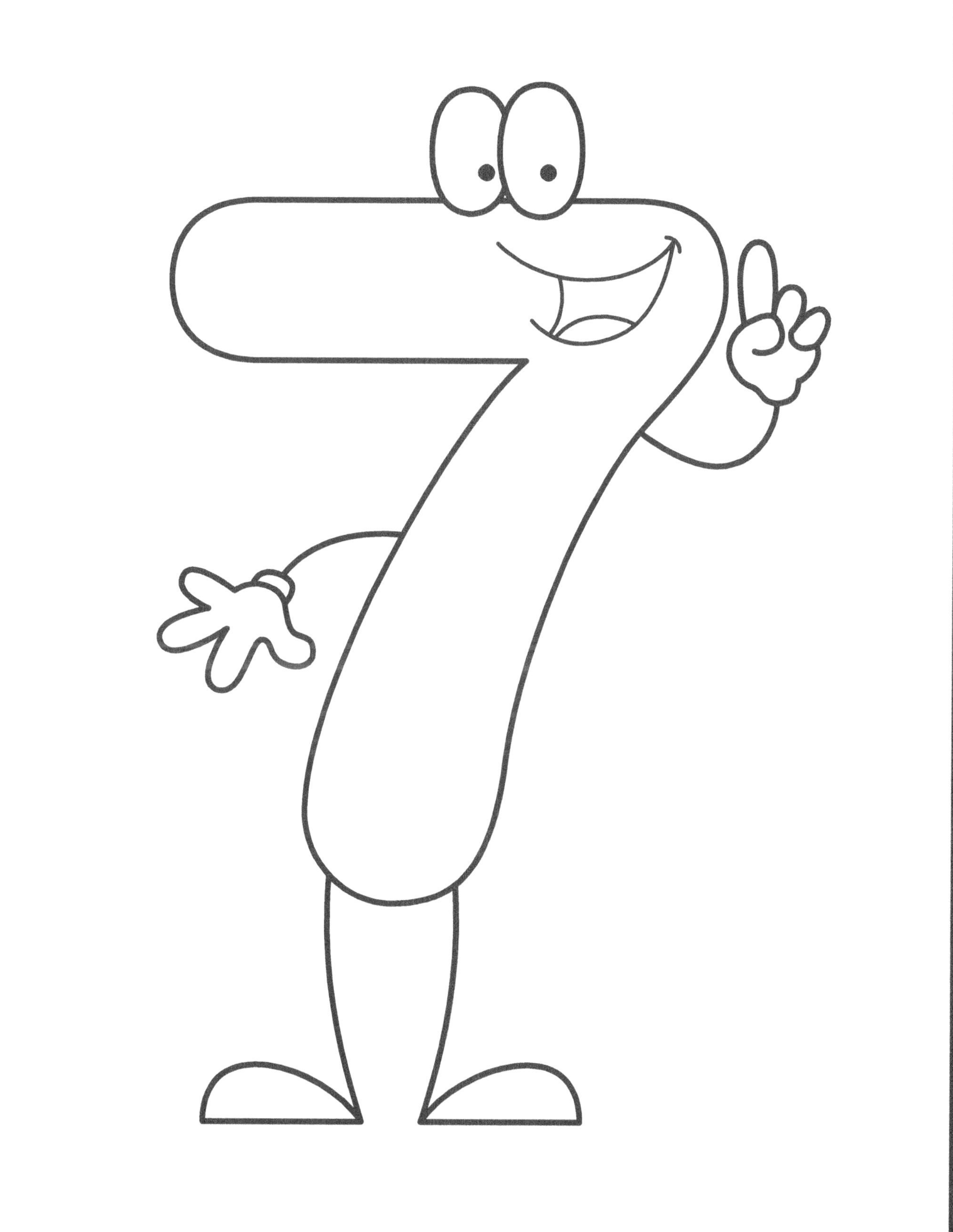

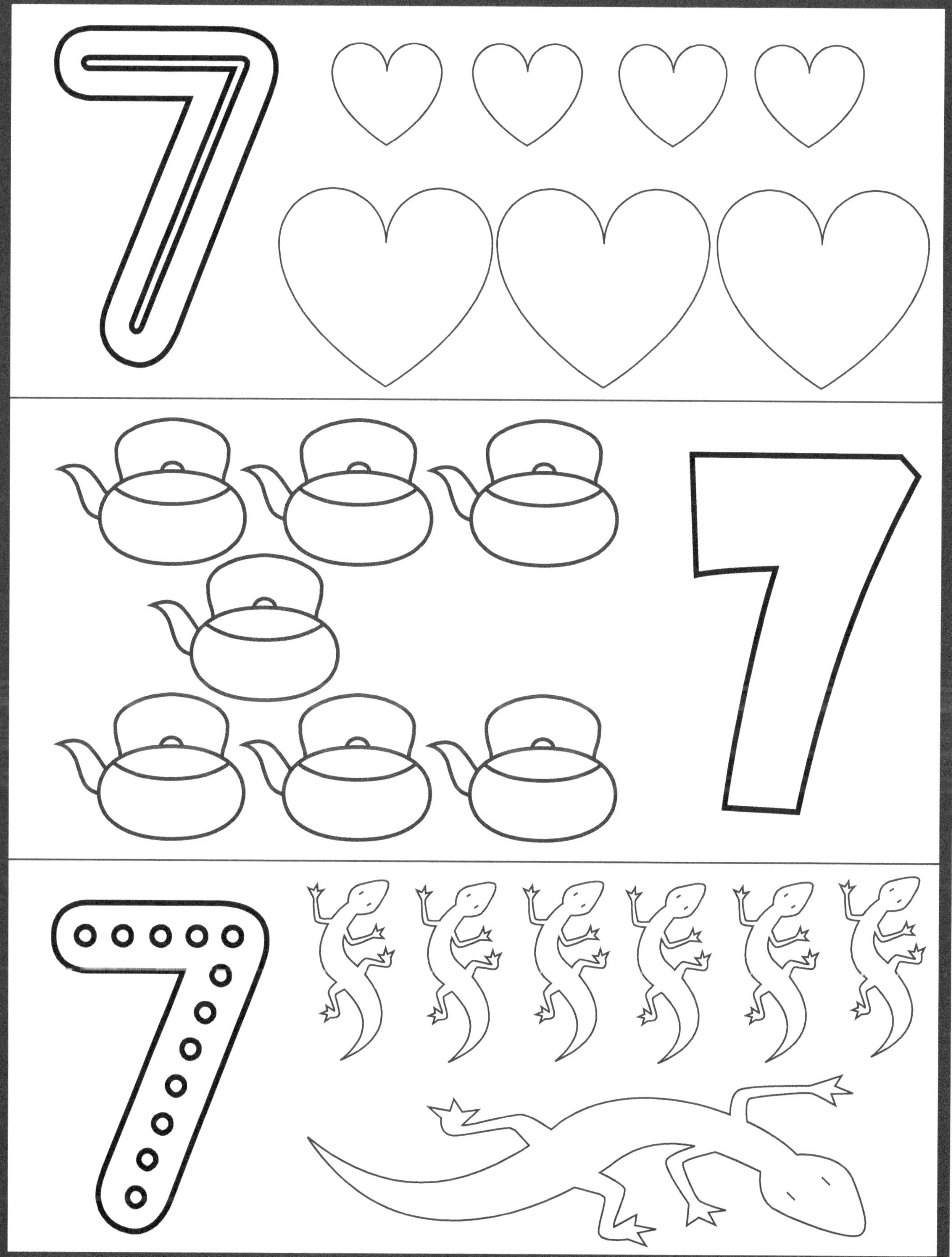

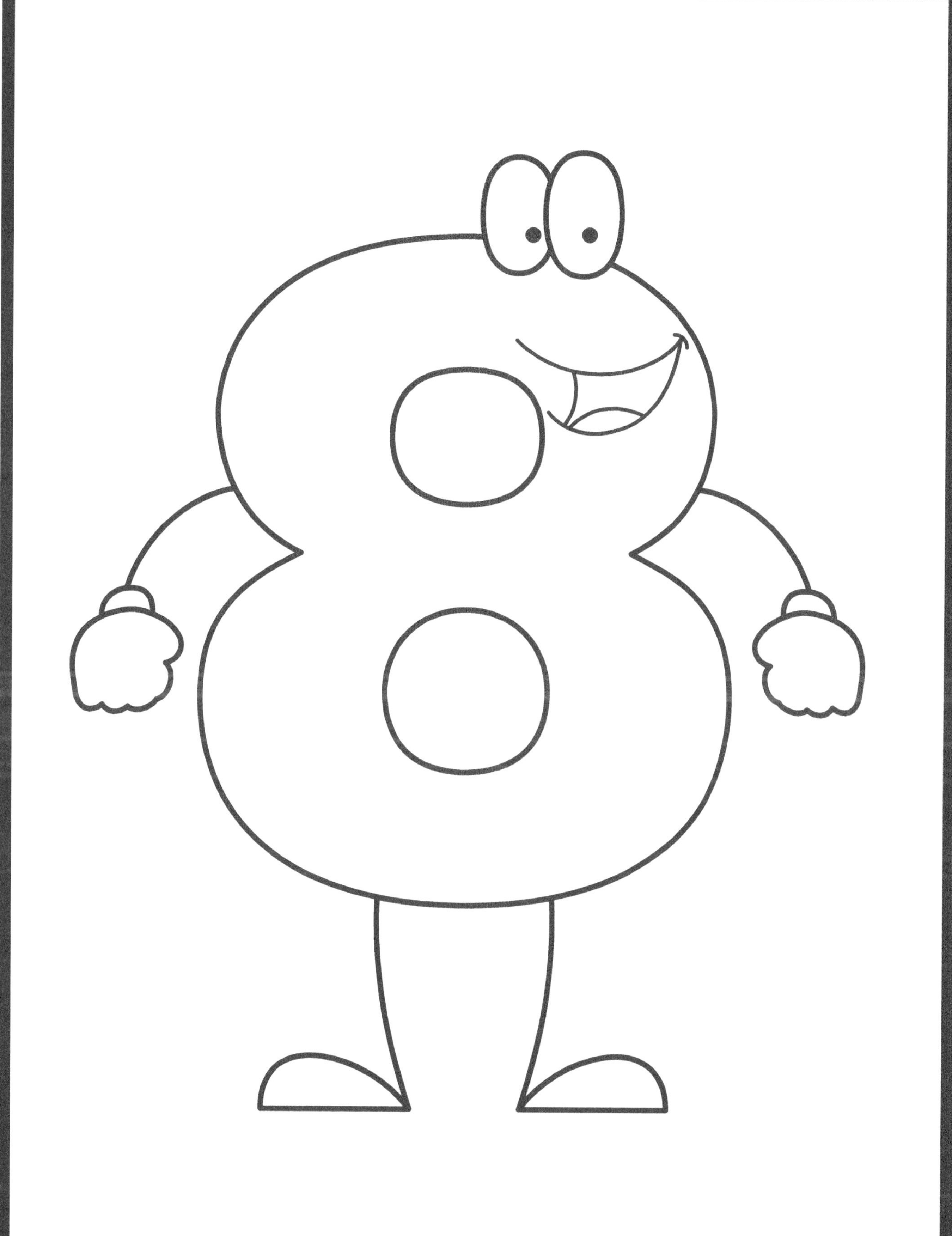

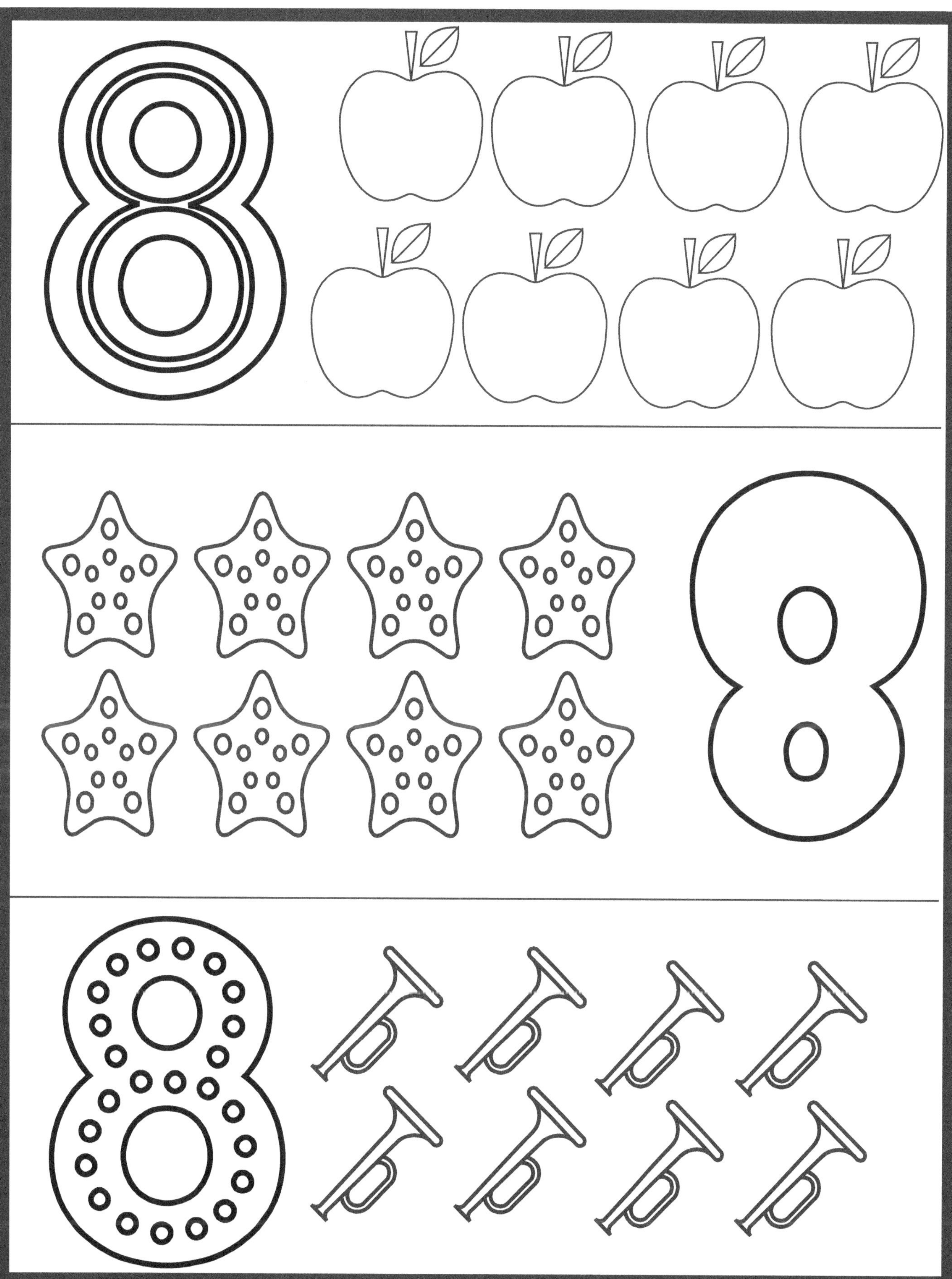

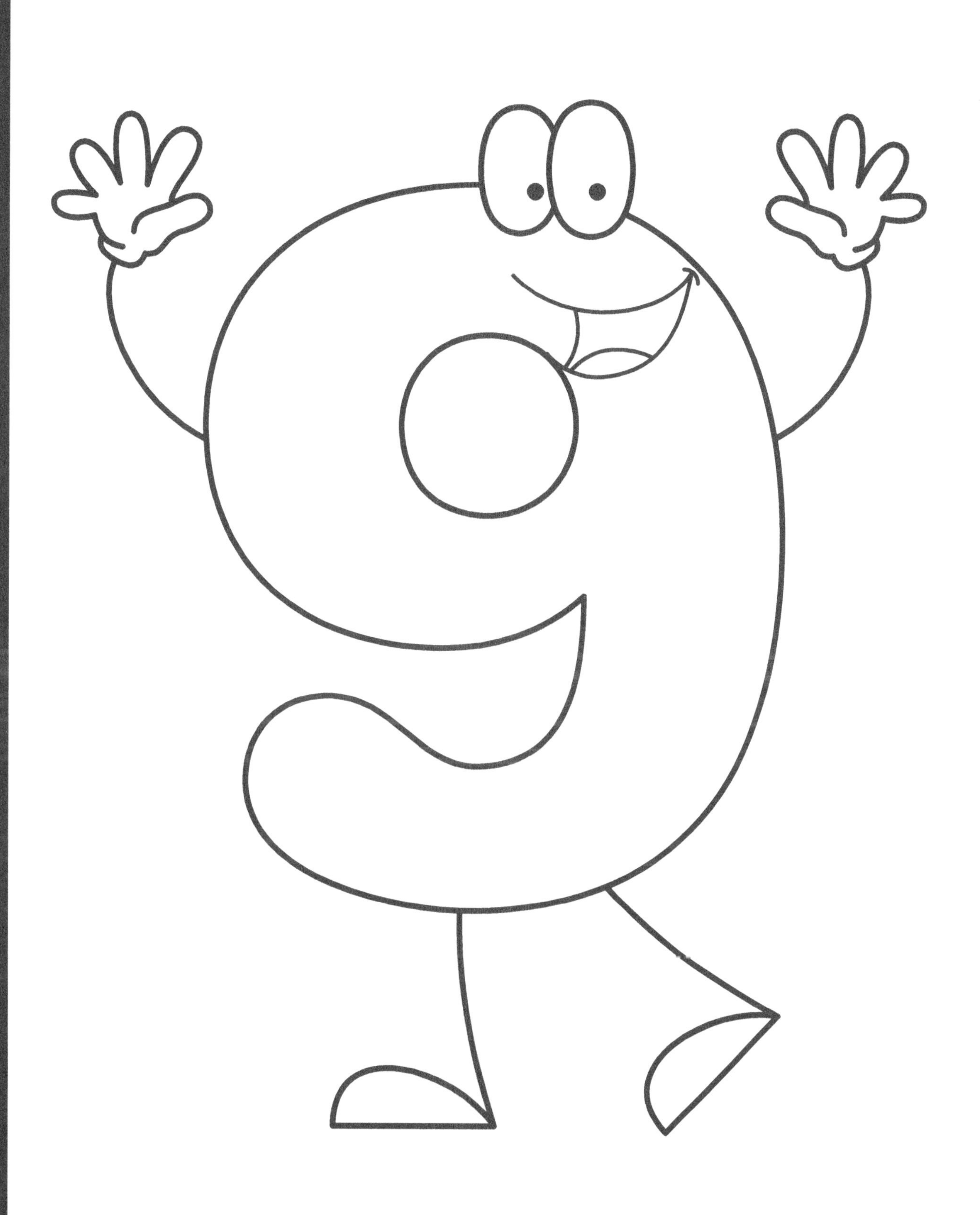

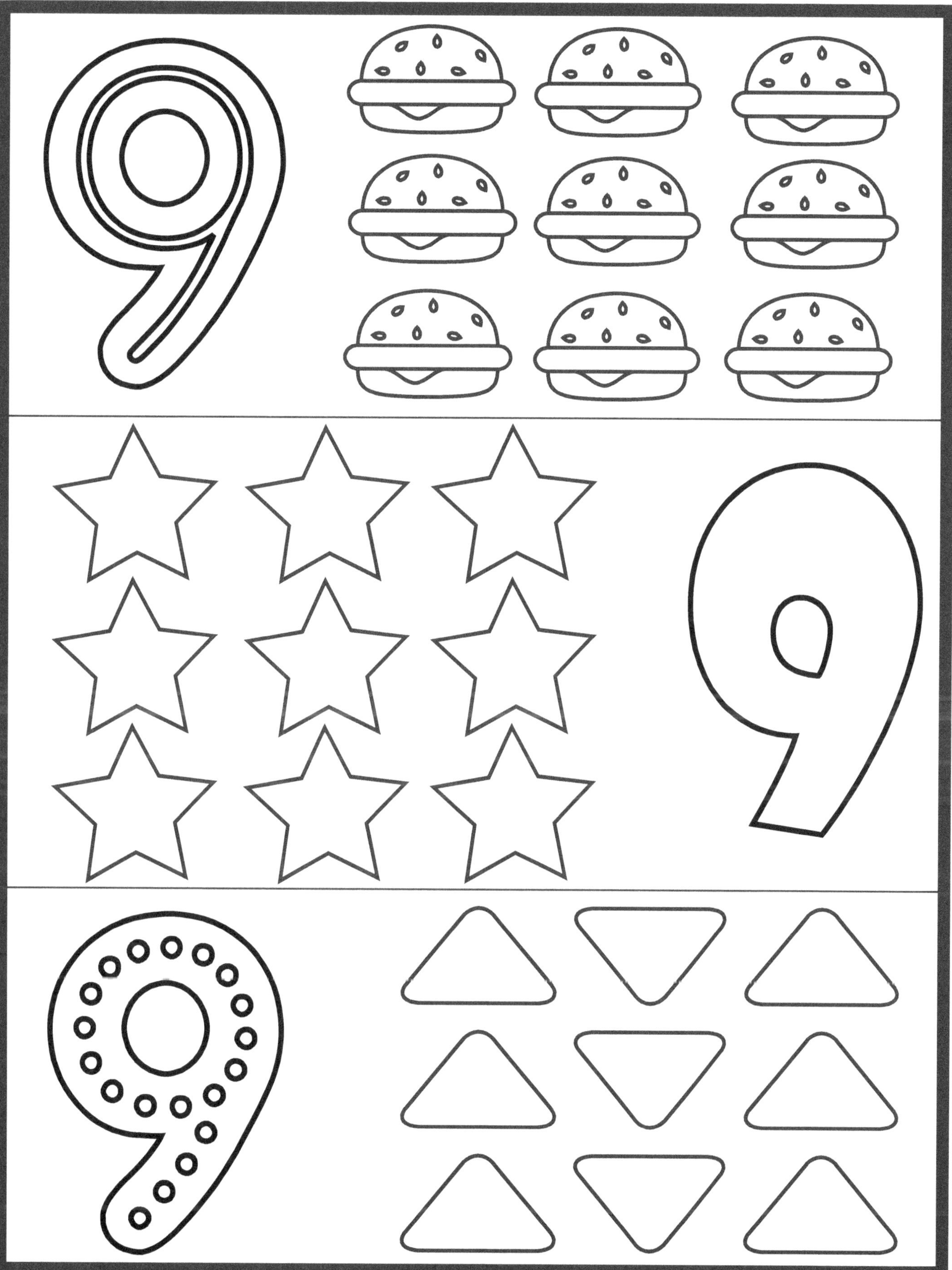

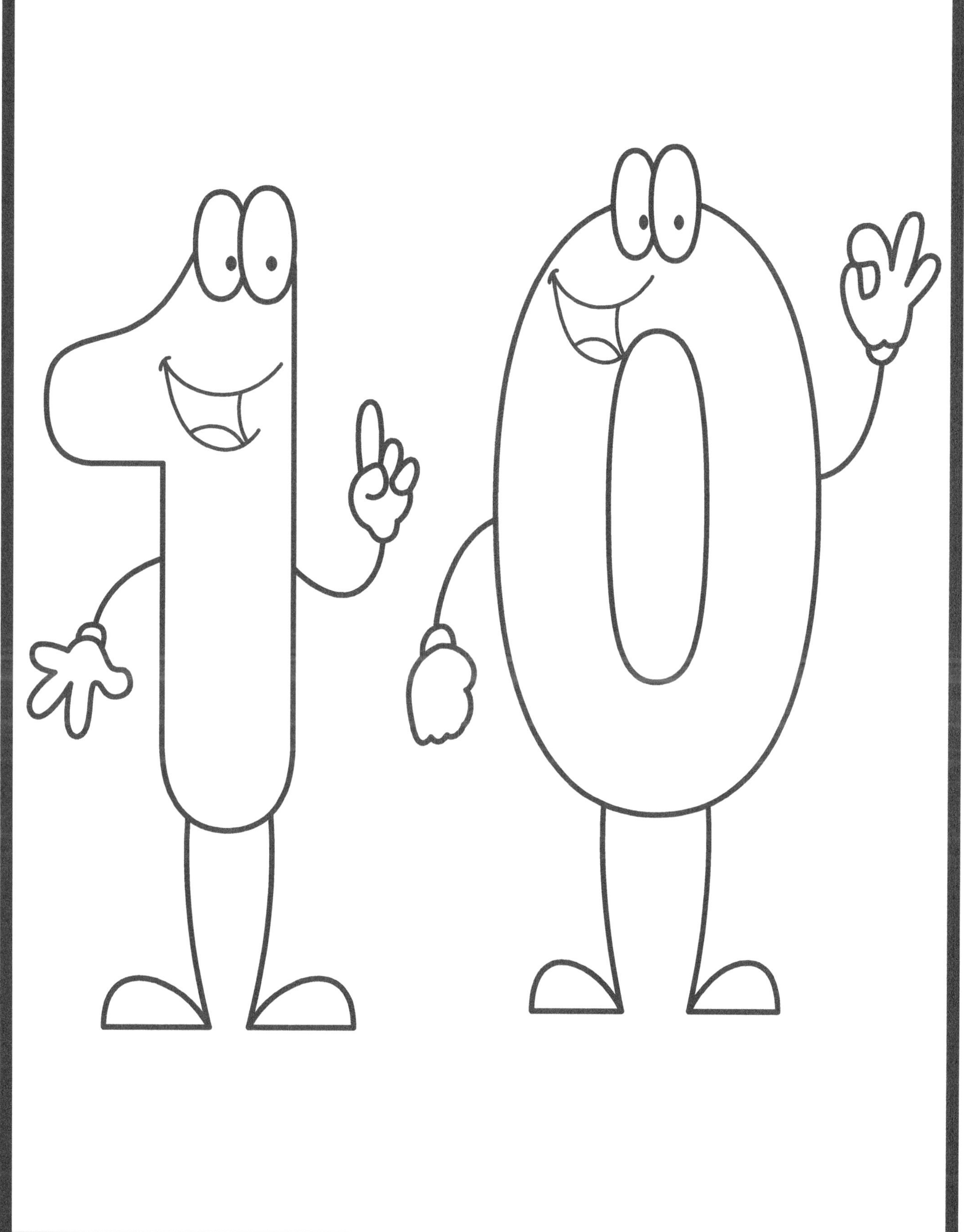

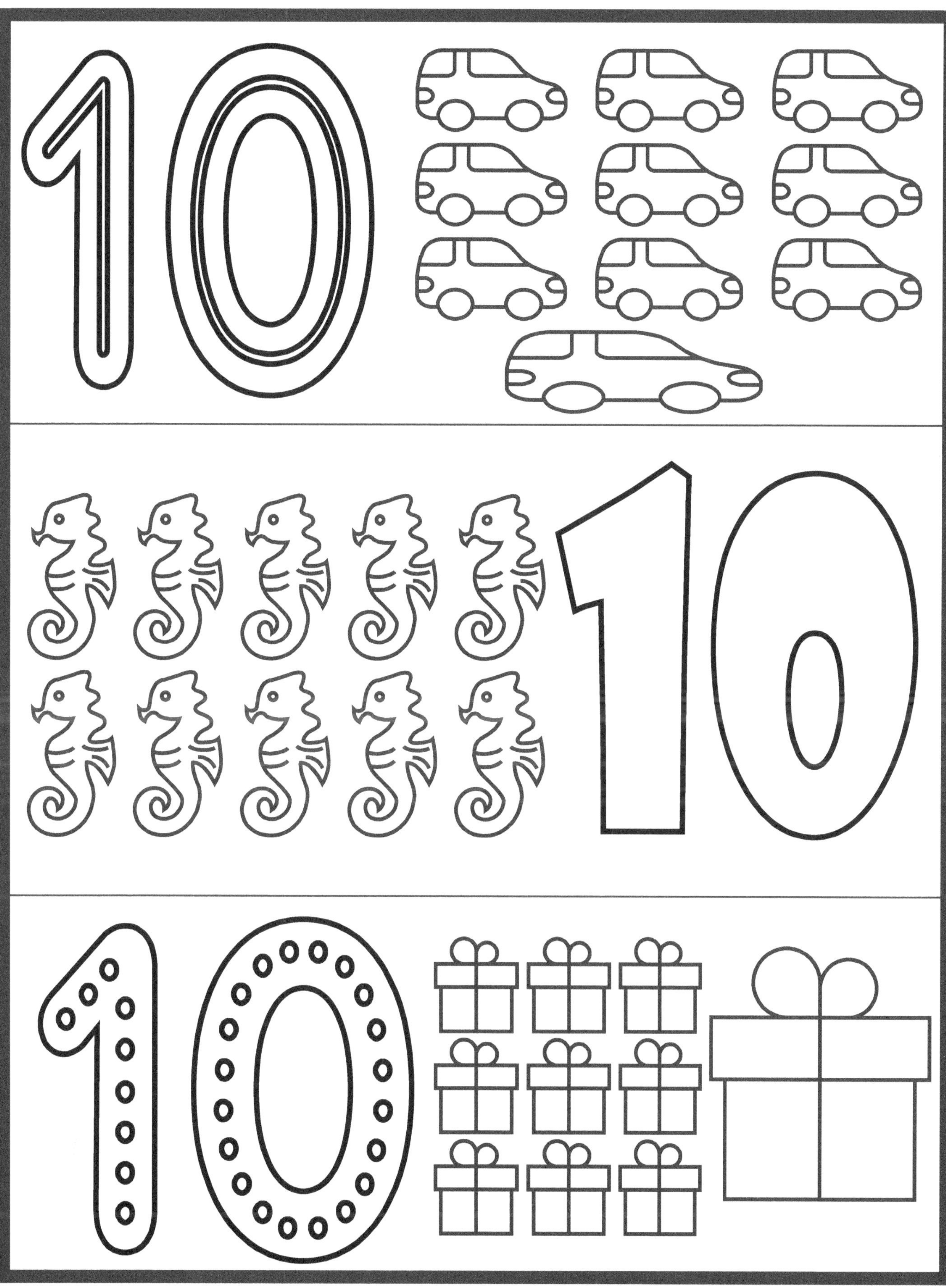

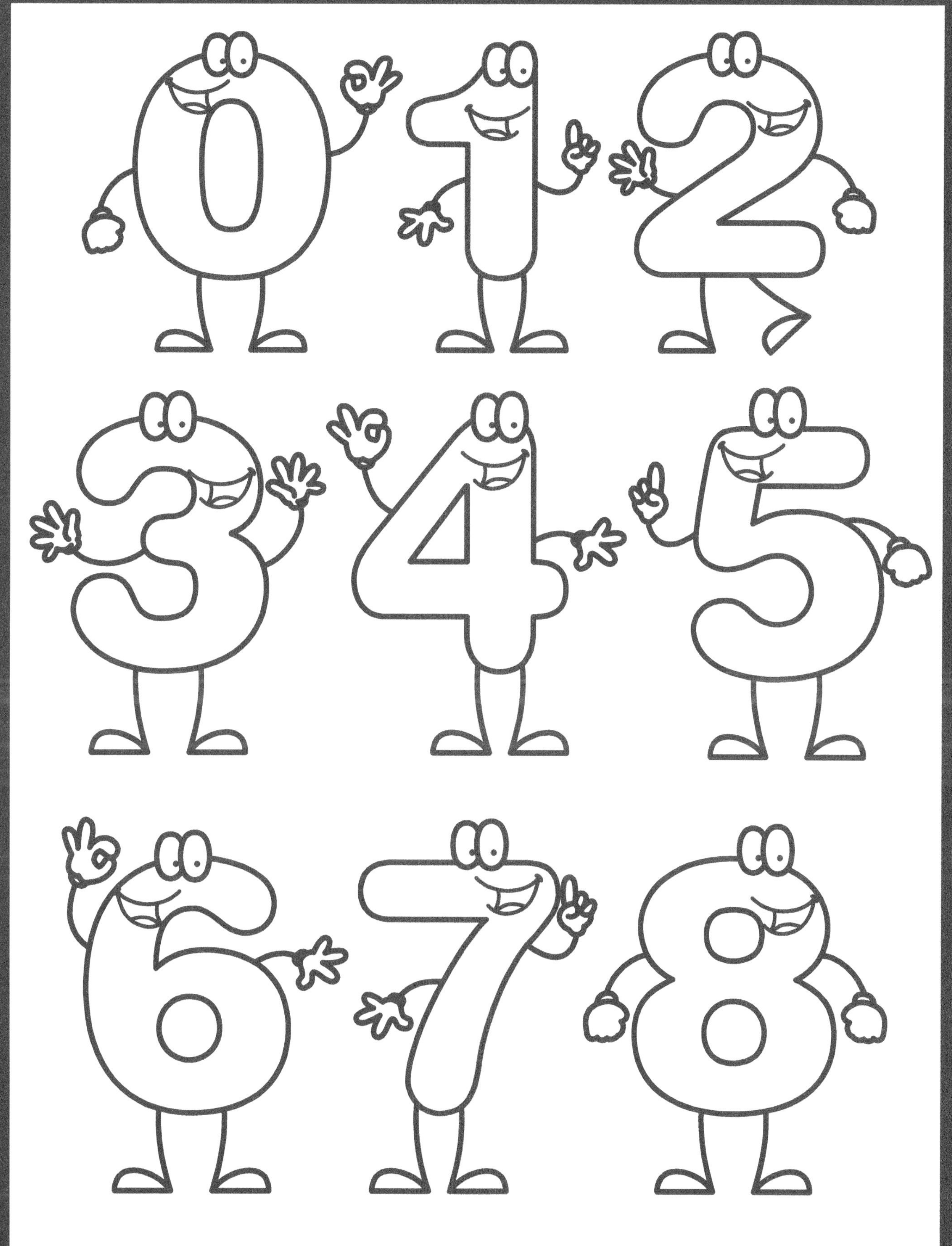

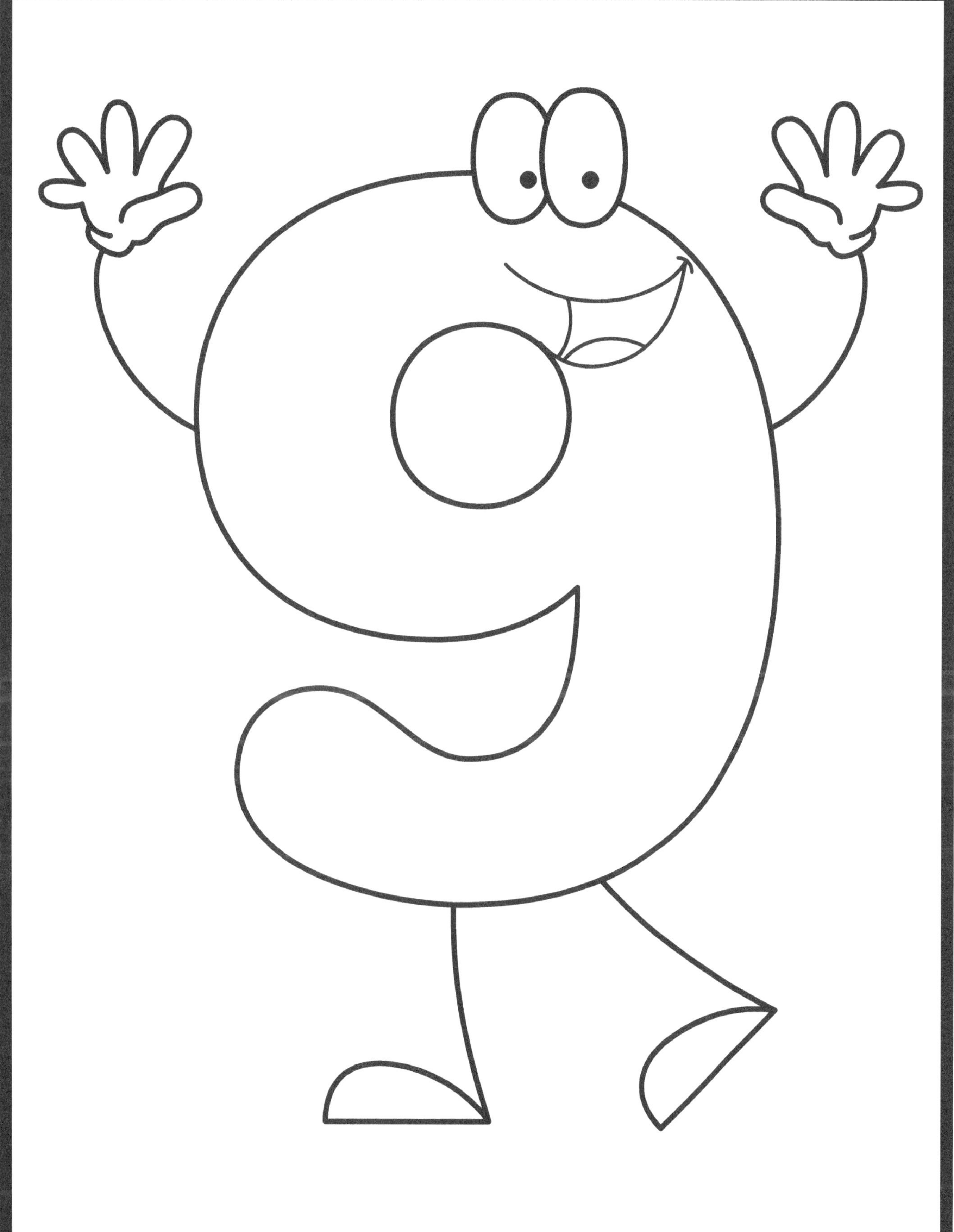

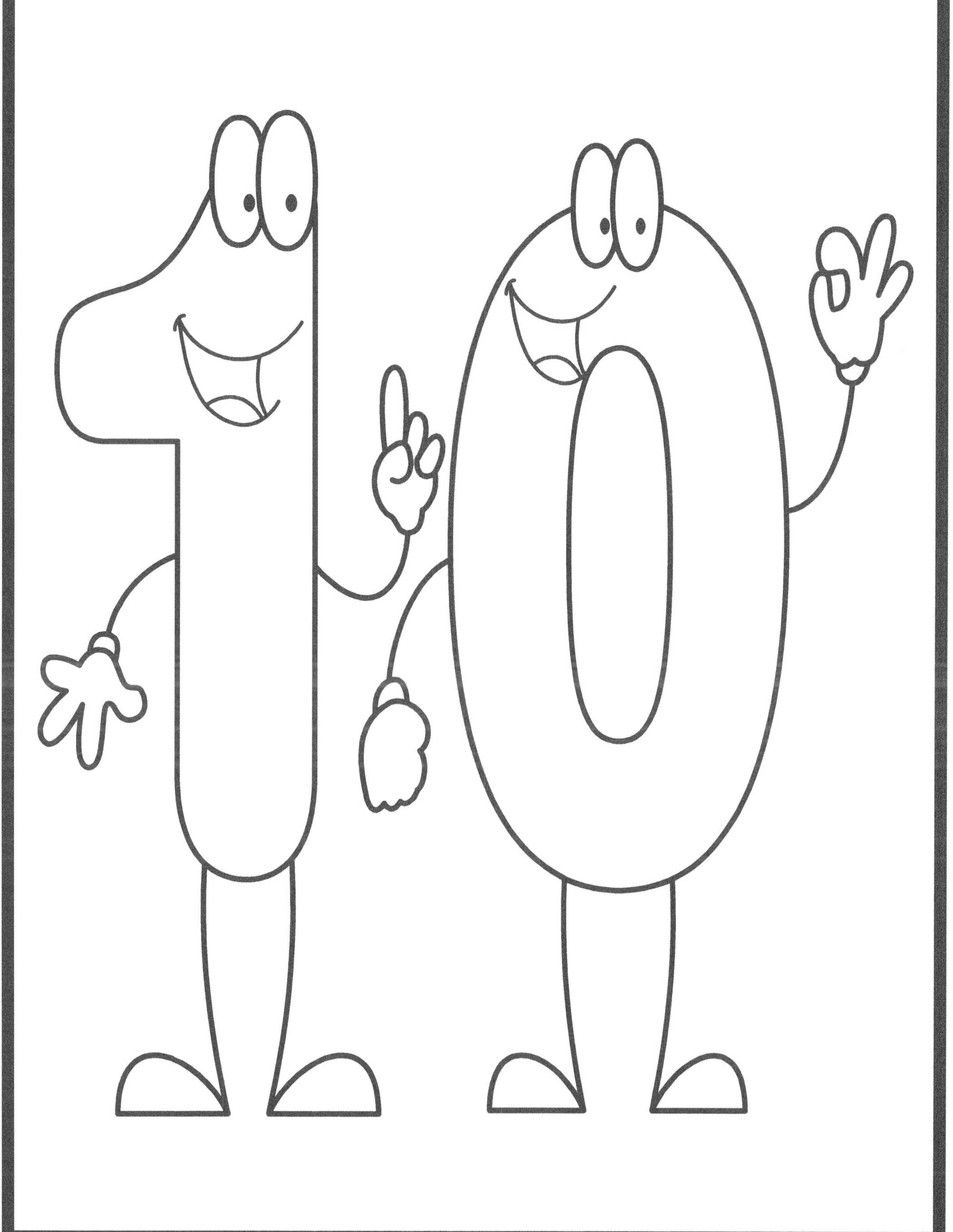